GYMNASTICS
BALANCE BEAM AND FLOOR EXERCISES

JOANNE MATTERN

The Rourke Corporation, Inc.
Vero Beach, Florida 32964

PROJECT EDITOR:
Genger Thorn is a professional member of USA and AAU gymnastics associations. She is USA safety certified and an associate member of the US Elite Coaches Association (USECA). Genger is currently a girls team coach and director at East Coast Gymnastics, Merritt Island, Florida.

PHOTO CREDITS: All photos Tony Gray except page 4 © Archive photo

DESIGNED BY: East Coast Studios, Merritt Island, Florida

EDITORIAL SERVICES:
Janice L. Smith for Penworthy Learning Systems

Library of Congress Cataloging-in-Publication Data

Mattern, Joanne, 1963-
  Gymnastics / by Joanne Mattern
    p. cm.
  Includes bibliographical references and indexes.
  Contents: [1] Training and fitness — [2] The pommel horse and the rings — [3] The vault — [4] Balance beam and floor exercises — [5] Uneven parallel bars — [6] Parallel bars and horizontal bar.
  ISBN 0-86593-571-8 (v.1). — ISBN 0-86593-568-8 (v. 2). — ISBN 0-86593-566-1 (v. 3). — ISBN 0-86593-567.X (v. 4). — ISBN 0-86593-569-6 (v. 5). — ISBN 0-86593-570-X (v. 6)
  1. Gymnastics for children Juvenile literature. [1. Gymnastics.] I. Title
GV464.5.M38 1999
796.44—dc21   99-27924
                                                            CIP

Printed in the USA

TABLE OF CONTENTS

Daniela Silvas performing at the 1988 Olympic games

CHAPTER ONE

GRACE IN MOTION

Floor exercises and the balance beam are two different gymnastics events. But gymnasts in both events exhibit many of the same skills. In each event, the gymnast tries to show as much grace, flexibility, balance, and strength as possible.

In competitive gymnastics there are ten levels of competition. In levels 1 through 6, there are **compulsory** (kum PAWLSS uh ree) **routines** (roo TEENZ). All of the gymnasts perform the same routines with the same music. At levels 7 through 10 the coach and gymnast create a routine on bars, beam, and floor with each skill having an assigned value. A back walkover, for example, is currently rated as an "A" skill on the balance beam. These ratings go to "E" for the most difficult moves. At levels 7 through 10 the gymnast is expected to perform a number of skills. A level 7 beam routine must contain "A" and "B" skills, but no "C" skills are required. If an unrequired skill is done, the judges will void the routine and a score of 0.00 will be given.

Only women use music to accompany their floor exercises. A gymnast's choice of music and moves gives her routine a unique style. Men also compete on the floor but not on the balance beam.

TOP VIEW OF SPRING FLOOR

40 feet (12.2 m)

40 feet (12.2 m)

END VIEW OF BALANCE BEAM

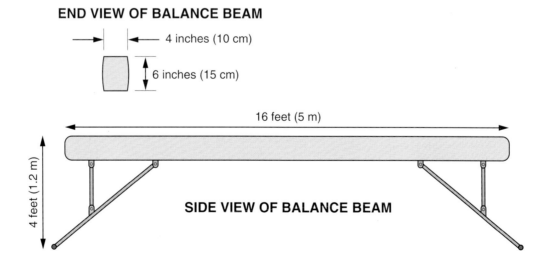

4 inches (10 cm)

6 inches (15 cm)

16 feet (5 m)

4 feet (1.2 m)

SIDE VIEW OF BALANCE BEAM

About Floor Exercises

Thirty years ago, floor exercises were performed on a hard wooden floor. Later, gymnasts were allowed to place small **mats** (MATS) in the corners. These mats were used for tumbling. But because the mats covered such a small area, the gymnasts could not perform very dramatic routines.

In time, mats covered the entire performance surface. This area is about 40 feet (12 meters) square. Today gymnasts compete on a **spring floor** (SPRING FLAWR). A spring floor consists of springs attached to plywood with foam padding on top covered by a large carpet. Spring floors allow the gymnast to perform more difficult and dazzling routines.

BASIC TUMBLING
AND BALANCING

Tumbling and balancing are the two most important skills a gymnast can have, because they are used in every gymnastic activity. This chapter covers some basic moves you can use in both floor and balance beam work.

Forward Roll

To do a forward roll:

1. Squat and place your hands on the floor about 18 inches (45 cm) in front of your feet. Your palms should be down and your fingers pointing straight ahead.
2. Straighten your legs and push forward with your feet.
3. As you roll forward, tuck your chin against your chest. Roll smoothly onto your shoulders and down your back.
4. As you roll onto your back, bring your hands up and grasp your shins. Pull your knees against you into a **tuck** (TUK) position.
5. When your feet touch the mat, push upward into a standing position.

Once you master the forward roll, trying doing a series of rolls, one after the other!

★ **COACH'S CORNER**

Getting Stuck!

Many beginning gymnasts stop when the backward roll reaches their shoulders, because they don't have enough momentum to keep moving. Solve this problem by rolling faster and pushing harder with your hands. Keeping your body in a tight tuck position will also help you complete the roll.

Forward roll

A straight-leg forward roll

Backward Roll

1. The backward roll starts in the same position as the forward roll. But instead of pushing forward with your feet, push back with your hands.
2. As you roll through a sitting position, put your chin against your chest, and roll onto your back.
3. As soon as your back touches the floor, move your hands to a point just above your shoulders. Place your palms on the floor with your fingers pointing backward.
4. Bend your legs into a tuck.
5. When the roll reaches your shoulders, push your hands hard against the floor to push yourself over and into a squatting position. Then move smoothly into a standing position.

Straight-Leg Forward Roll

For a straight-leg forward roll:

1. Start from a standing position, bend forward so that your palms are on the floor and your knees are slightly bent.
2. Bend your chin to your chest and push yourself into a forward roll. But for a straight-leg forward roll, don't tuck your legs against your body—keep them straight with your toes pointing backward.
3. As you roll down your back, push up with your hands. Keep your legs together as they move between your arms.
4. When your feet touch the floor, rise to a standing position.

Forward Straddle Roll

To do a forward straddle roll:

1. Bend forward from a standing position with your chin against your chest. Keep your legs as far apart as you can, and place your hands on the floor between your feet.

2. Bend your arms and roll forward onto your shoulders.

3. As you roll down your back, keep your legs far apart. Move your arms straight out in front as the roll reaches your hips and you move into a sitting position.

4. Drop your hands to the floor between your legs and push yourself into a standing position.

Performing a forward straddle roll (step 4)

Backward Straddle Roll

1. Start in the same position as for the forward straddle roll.
2. Support yourself on your hands as you drop your seat to the floor. Then roll onto your back without stopping.
3. Keep rolling until you reach your feet. Bring your hands alongside your shoulders to push yourself into a standing position.

Front Walkover

It's important to have a **spotter** (SPAHT er) to help you learn the front walkover.

1. First, stand up straight, stretch your arms over your head, and step forward with your right leg. You may feel more comfortable using your left leg.
2. Lunge forward until the palms of your hands touch the floor. At the same time, push forward and up with your lead leg.
3. As your hands reach the floor, bring your back leg over your head, arch your body, and allow your leg to continue down to the floor.
4. Straighten your body with your arms over your head and bring your leg to the floor.

This routine can be reversed to perform a back walkover.

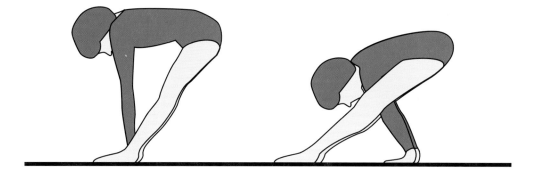

A backward straddle roll

Handstand

The handstand is one of the most difficult exercises in beginning gymnastics, as well as one of the most important skills in many events. So be sure to work with a spotter.

1. Start from a standing position, with one leg in front of the other. Lunge forward until your hands touch the floor. Spread your fingers and point them forward, with your palms firmly against the floor. Your arms should be straight and your shoulders should be directly over your fingertips.

2. Look at a spot on the floor about 12 inches (30 cm) in front of you. Keep your eyes on that spot as you kick up and back with your back leg. This will keep your head from dropping forward and throwing off your balance.

3. Follow your back leg with your lead leg until both legs are together and in a vertical position directly above your shoulders. Your body should be straight.

4. Once you reach the handstand position, adjust your hands to keep your balance. The more you practice, the easier it will be to get your balance on the first try.

Headstand

1. Squat and place your hands shoulder-width apart, about 12 inches (30 cm) in front of your knees. Your fingers should be facing out slightly.

2. Drop to your knees and lower your head to the floor about 12 inches (30 cm) in front of your hands. Your weight should be just above your forehead. Your hands and head will create a triangle-shaped base. You must keep your weight evenly balanced between your hands and head to achieve a successful headstand.

3. Lift your hips until your back is straight. Hold your legs parallel to the floor, with your knees bent and your toes pointing up.

4. Once your hips are over your shoulders, straighten your legs.

★ **COACH'S CORNER**

Headstands from a Standing Position

Place one foot in front of the other and lean forward until your head and hands form a triangle-shaped base. Then kick your back leg up. Your other leg should immediately follow into a vertical position.

Performing a headstand

Cartwheel

1. Stand with your left foot slightly in front of your right and your arms stretched up and out.

2. Rock onto your right foot, then back to your left. As you move onto your left foot, bend from your waist to the left.

3. Place your left palm flat on the floor about two feet (just over .5 m) in front of your left foot. At the same time, swing your right leg up and push off from the floor with your left foot.

4. As both legs swing over your head, place your right hand on the floor and shift your weight onto it. To keep your balance, focus on a spot about 12 inches (30 cm) behind your hands.

5. Bend at the waist and aim your right foot toward the floor.

6. Swing your left foot down. Your upper body will follow until you end in a standing position, feet apart (the same position you started in). You can perform a cartwheel by leading with either your left or right foot.

Round Off

1. Take several running steps and reach forward by placing your right hand on the floor.

2. As your body turns to the left, place your left hand on the floor. Simultaneously kick your left leg.

3. Pass through a side handstand. After your feet pass verticle, bring your legs together and turn 90 degrees to the left.

4. Push explosively off the floor with your arms and shoulders while snapping your legs down to land on the floor. You can also reverse these directions and use your other leg.

5. Lunge back with your back leg and lift your arms overhead.

Performing a back bend

Back Bend

1. Lie flat on your back with your knees together and bent. Place your hands alongside your shoulders with your fingers pointed toward the shoulders and your elbows pointing straight up into the air.

2. Press your hands and feet against the floor. Keep the top of your head against the floor and arch your back as deeply as you can. This position is called a back bridge.

3. Straighten your arms and bring your head up. Your body should be in a high, deep arch from your hands to your feet.

Back Handspring

Also known as a flic-flac, the back handspring can be used during floor exercises and on the balance beam.

1. With both legs together, push explosively off the floor with your arms and shoulders while simultaneously snapping your legs down and under to land on both feet in an upright **hollow** (HAHL O) position.

This move is learned in parts and should be mastered before competition.

★	COACH'S CORNER

Little by Little

Try to deepen the arch of your back each time you practice a back bend. But don't stretch more than a little each day, or your muscles will be very sore!

DANCE MOVES

Along with tumbling, balance beam routines and floor exercises also require dancing movements.

Leaps and Jumps

This section describes some basic **leaps** (LEEPS) and **jumps** (JUMPS).

Cat Jump

1. Stand with your right foot in front of your left with your feet turned out.
2. Jump with your left foot and bend your right knee out to the side. Then bend your left knee out. Both feet should pass close to each other while you're in the air. This jump is called a cat jump.

23

Tuck Jump

To do a tuck jump:

1. Start with your feet together. As you jump straight up, drop your head forward, bend your knees, and bring them close to your face.

2. Swing your arms high and back.

3. Land on the balls of both feet.

Running Leap

1. This leap starts with you running two or three steps to build up momentum.

2. Push off with your back foot and stretch your front leg forward while extending your back leg back. Keep your toes pointed.

3. Hold your back straight as you move through the air. Your arms should be extended front and back, the same way your legs are.

Stag Jump

To do a stag jump:

1. Start by running two or three steps. Then take off from one foot and leap as high as you can.

2. As you travel through the air, extend the back leg out straight. At the same time, bend the knee of your front leg so your foot is close to the thigh of your back leg. Extend your arms front and back or to the sides.

⭐ **COACH'S CORNER**

Takeoffs and Landings

As you practice your leaps, don't always use the same foot for takeoffs or landings. Practice until you are comfortable taking off and landing on either foot.

A running leap

Performing a front scale

Poses and Balances

In addition to leaps and jumps, a gymnast needs to learn dance movements called **poses** (POZ ez). The front **scale** (SKAYL) is the most basic pose.

Front Scale

1. Stand on one leg, with your foot flat on the floor.
2. Lean your upper body forward until it is parallel to the floor.
3. Raise your other leg behind you until your foot is above your head. The toes on this foot should be pointed.
4. There should be an **arch** (AHRCH), or curve, in your body, running from the top of your raised foot to the top of your head. Be sure to keep your head high and your arms out to the side for balance.

Miscellaneous Skills

Other skills can greatly enhance a gymnast's routines. To do a plié:

Plié

1. Step forward with your toes pointed and your arms swinging freely at your sides.
2. On each step, dip slightly by bending your knees. If this step is performed on the balance beam, one foot should drop below the level of the beam.

Pivot Turn

1. Stand with one foot about six inches (15 cm) in front of the other.
2. Rise onto the balls of both feet and spin halfway around, so you are looking in the opposite direction from where you started.
3. At the end of the pivot, or turn, drop your heels to the floor.

Kick Turn

To execute a kick turn:

1. Step forward onto your right foot. Keep your arms arched gracefully over your head.

2. Swing one leg to the front, extending it high and straight. Then swing the same leg to the rear, again in a high, straight position.

3. As your leg swings to the rear, pivot with your other foot until you are turned in the opposite direction from where you started. Always pivot in the direction of the turn. For example, if your left leg is extended, pivot to the left.

Almost any move in ballet, jazz, or other forms of dance may be added to a routine. Dance adds elegance and rhythm and makes your routine more interesting and complete.

THE BALANCE BEAM

The balance beam is the only **apparatus** (AP uh RAT uhs) developed just for women gymnasts. The beam was invented in Sweden and was first used in the 1800s. It is made of wood, or metal, and measures just over 16 feet (5 m) long. It is four feet (1.2 m) high and four inches (10 cm) wide. The newer beams are metal and have a thin layer of padding and a non-slip covering. By giving the gymnast better footing, it helps prevent injury.

A balance beam routine lasts between 1 minute, 15 seconds and 1 minute, 35 seconds. During the routine, the gymnast must perform walking and running steps, **balances** (BAL uns ez), jumps, leaps, turns, and poses, while using the beams entire length as well as extending above and getting low on the beam.

Posture Makes Perfect

You must have correct posture to keep your balance and perform a graceful routine on the beam. Hold your body straight and tall, with your head high and your shoulders relaxed. Your back should be straight and relaxed, and your hips should be tucked forward so that you are standing erect. Keep your weight directly over your feet and don't lean to one side.

Practice balancing skills on a low beam before trying the balance beam.

Posture, hand positions, and foot positions—remember and practice all of them.

As you walk, keep your legs straight (except when a movement requires you to bend your knees) and your feet pointed out slightly. Always keep your toes pointed forward. Your arms should move freely as you walk to help you keep your balance. Most of all, keep a tall, confident attitude!

Getting Started

You can't just hop up on the balance beam on your first day at the gym. It's important to work on your balancing skills on the ground first! Mark a four-inch-wide (10-cm-wide) line on the floor with chalk or masking tape. Practice walking along this line, both forward and backward, until you have no trouble keeping your balance. Then move up to a bench and try your movements there.

★ **DID YOU KNOW?**

Differences Between Men and Women

A woman's floor exercise lasts from 60 to 90 seconds. Her routine is judged on grace and balance, and should flow like a dance routine. Women compete to music, but men do not.

A man has 50 to 70 seconds to perform his floor routine. His routine contains more acrobatic elements and is judged more for displays of strength than a woman's routine is.

When you're finally ready to get on the beam, set it just one or two feet (.3 or .6 m) off the floor. Make sure you have pads around the base of the beam. Once you've had enough practice, you can move the beam up to its full height.

Ask a coach to help you when you try new moves.

A front-support mount—one of the most basic mounts

Hands and Feet

The position of your hands and feet is very important as you move along the beam. Keep your feet turned out for better balance, and place your weight on the balls of your feet. When performing a skill like the handstand or walkover you should keep your palms flat on the beam, with your fingers extended over the sides of the beam.

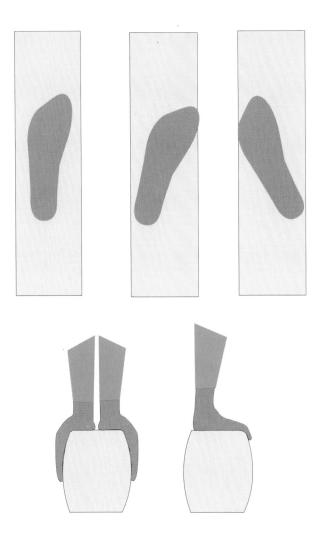

MOUNTS AND DISMOUNTS

Before you practice your tumbling, poses, and dance moves on the balance beam, you need to learn how to get on, or **mount** (MOUNT), and how to get off or **dismount** (DISS MOUNT). A strong mount will get you off to a good start, and a graceful dismount will leave the judges with a good impression. Often, the dismount is the high point of the routine, as the gymnast performs a spectacular skill that leaves the audience cheering!

Mounts

Several mounts are described below, in order of basic to more advanced.

Front-Support Mount
1. Stand facing the side of the beam and grip the top with both hands.
2. Bend your knees and jump straight up, supporting yourself on your arms. Your arms and legs should be straight, with your thighs against the beam and your body arched slightly. Point your toes and hold your head high.
3. Swing one leg out to the side and bring it across the beam. At the same time, turn your body so that you are straddling the beam in a sitting position. Keep your weight on your hands until you sit on the beam.

Knee Mount
1. Stand facing the side of the beam and grip the top with both hands. Bend your knees and jump straight up, supporting yourself on your arms.
2. Bring one knee up until it is resting on the beam between your hands.
3. Swing your other leg back and up until your toes are just above your head.
4. Make a quarter turn so that you are facing the length of the beam. Drop your back foot onto the beam.

A knee mount

Squat Mount

1. Stand facing the side of the beam and grip the top with both hands for a squat mount. Bend your knees and jump straight up, supporting yourself on your arms.

2. Lift your seat and bend your knees as you position your feet on the beam between your hands. Hold your head high and straight to keep your balance.

Straddle Mount

1. The straddle mount starts the same way as the squat mount—jump straight onto the beam while supporting your weight with your hands.

2. Instead of bending your knees and placing your feet between your hands, stretch your legs out to the side so that your feet land outside your hands in the **straddle** (STRAD ul) position.

Jump Mount

You need a **springboard** (SPRING BAWRD) placed next to the beam to do the more advanced jump mount.

1. First, take a short run to the beam. Place your right foot on the springboard and swing your left leg up.

2. Keeping your arms forward, place your left foot on the beam with your knee bent.

3. Put your weight onto your left leg and stretch your right leg behind you.

4. Swing your right leg forward and straighten the left leg. Extend your left arm forward and your right arm back.

Forward Roll Mount

1. Using a springboard take a short run to the beam. Place your hands on the end of the beam and jump off the springboard, lifting your hips over your head.

2. Roll your head forward with your chin tucked against your chest. Place your head on the beam as close to your hands as possible.

3. Keeping your legs straight, roll forward until your seat touches the beam.

4. Move your hands behind your hips and keep your legs in front of you, toes pointing toward the ceiling. This should be practiced with a coach.

Dismounts

It's a good idea to practice jumping off the beam until you feel comfortable landing. Start by simply dropping feet-first off the beam onto a mat. Be sure to land on the balls of your feet.

★ COACH'S CORNER

Getting the Feel
of the Straddle Position

It's hard to get your balance in the straddle mount until you are comfortable with the straddle position itself. Work with a spotter and practice holding the straddle position on the beam until you feel comfortable and balanced. Then try the straddle mount.

When you land on the mat, bend your knees to absorb the impact. Then put your feet flat on the floor and straighten into a standing position. Competition rules specify that you must straighten your legs, drop your arms to your sides, and come to attention. If you don't, or if you hop or take an extra step to get your balance, the judges will lower your score.

Straddle Jump Dismount

To do a straddle jump dismount:

1. Stand on your toes with your arms out sideways.

2. Swing your arms down and bend your legs.

3. Stretch your legs and swing your arms up as you jump from the beam.

4. At the highest point of your jump, straddle your legs and bring your hands down to touch your toes.

5. Swing your arms up and bring your legs together so you are in a standing position in the air.

6. Land on your toes with your knees bent.

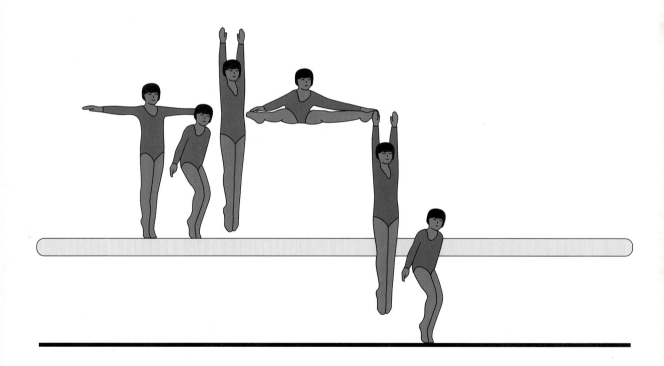

A handstand dismount

Arch Dismount

1. Stand on the beam facing sideways, with your legs straight and your arms stretched in front of you for an arch dismount.
2. Dip your knees and swing your arms down and back to propel yourself through the air.
3. Swing your arms high and back as you push off from the balls of your feet.
4. Arch your back deeply as you fly through the air. Land with your arms outstretched and knees bent.

Handstand Dismount

A more advanced dismount is the handstand dismount.
1. Starting from a handstand position, push off with your right (or left) hand and straighten your right (or left) arm.
2. Look down and focus on a landing spot.
3. Swing your legs up and over your head and let your body follow them.
4. Straighten your body before you land. Then bend your legs and land on your toes.

Front Tuck Off the End

The front tuck off the end of the beam is a difficult dismount that should be attempted only by very experienced gymnasts.
1. Take several running steps and punch off of both feet at the end of the beam.
2. Reach upward with your arms and tuck your knees to your chest as you rotate.
3. Open your tuck and straighten your body when you spot the floor. Land on slightly bent knees, then steady yourself and show a finished position.

GLOSSARY

apparatus (AP uh RAT uhs) — a special piece of equipment for performing a gymnastic event

arch (AHRCH) — a position where the upper and lower parts of your body form a slight curve

balance (BAL uns) — a pose that is held for more than just a moment

compulsory (kum PAWLSS uh ree) — a required routine or movement

dismount (DISS MOUNT) — to get off an apparatus

jump (JUMP) — a move that carries you straight up into the air

hollow (HAHL O) — a position where the body is stretched fully with a slightly rounded back

leap (LEEP) — a move that carries you through the air for a distance, either forward or backward

mat (MAT) — a padded surface that provides a soft, safe landing for a gymnast

mount (MOUNT) — to get on an apparatus

pose (POZ) — a position that is held just for a moment

routine (roo TEEN) — a combination of moves displaying a full range of skills

scale (SKAYL) — a balance on one leg

GLOSSARY

spotter (SPAHT er) — a coach or experienced gymnast who stands below a gymnast to give advice and catch him or her in the event of a fall

springboard (SPRING BAWRD) — a flexible board used to help a gymnast jump high in the air; also called a beatboard or Reuther board

spring floor (SPRING FLAWR) — a special surface made of plywood and rubber with springs underneath to give the gymnast extra power in the floor exercise and allow him or her to perform difficult and challenging skills

straddle (STRAD ul) — a position in which the legs are held straight and apart across an apparatus

tuck (TUK) — a position in which the knees and hips are bent and drawn into the chest

FURTHER READING

Find out more about floor exercises and the balance beam from these helpful books, magazines, and information sites:

- Dolan, Edward F., Jr. *The Complete Beginner's Guide to Gymnastics.* Garden City, NY: Doubleday & Company, Inc., 1980.
- Feeney, Rik. *Gymnastics: A Guide for Parents and Athletes.* Indianapolis: Masters Press, 1992.
- Gutman, Dan. *Gymnastics.* New York: Viking, 1996.
- Marks, Marjorie. *A Basic Guide to Gymnastics: An Official U.S. Olympic Committee Sports Series.* Glendale, CA: Griffin Publishing, 1998.
- Murdock, Tony and Nik Stuart. *Gymnastics: A Practical Guide for Beginners.* New York: Franklin Watts, 1980.
- Peszek, Luan. *The Gymnastics Almanac.* Los Angeles: Lowell House, 1998.
- *USA Gymnastics Safety Handbook.* Indianapolis: USA Gymnastics, 1998.

- *USA Gymnastics*—This magazines covers American competitions and athletes, as well as major competitions leading up to the Olympics.
- *Technique*—This publication is geared toward coaches and judges.
- *International Gymnast*—This magazine covers both American and international competitions and athletes.

- www.usa-gymnastics.org
  This is the official Website of USA Gymnastics, the national governing body for gymnastics in the United States.
- www.ngja.org
  National Gymnastics Judges Association, Inc.
- www.ngja.org
  This is the official Website for the National Gymnastics Judges Association, Inc.

INDEX